THE SCOUTS

Susan Cohen

Published in Great Britain in 2012 by Shire Publications
Ltd, Midland House, West Way, Botley, Oxford OX2 0PH,
United Kingdom.

44-02 23rd Street, Suite 219, Long Island City, NY 11101,
USA.

E-mail: shire@shirebooks.co.uk   www.shirebooks.co.uk

A CIP catalogue record for this book is available from the
British Library.

Shire Library no. 690.   ISBN-13: 978 0 74781 151 0

Susan Cohen has asserted her right under the Copyright,
Designs and Patents Act, 1988, to be identified as the
author of this book.

Designed by Tony Truscott Designs, Sussex, UK
and typeset in Perpetua and Gill Sans.

Printed in China through Worldprint Ltd.

12 13 14 15 16   10 9 8 7 6 5 4 3 2 1

COVER IMAGE
From the front cover of a special Hiking and Scouting
edition of *The Scout*, showing two enthusiastic and earnest
boy scouts reading a map while on a hike, *c.* 1934. ©
Mary Evans.

TITLE PAGE IMAGE
An Irish Scout in camp washing himself before morning
inspection in 1966. The boys brought the buckets and
basins with them and made the washstand-cum-clothes
dryer with materials available on the campsite.

ACKNOWLEDGEMENTS
My thanks to The Scout Association, and to Daniel Scott-
Davies, Archivist and Heritage Manager, for the provision
of research material and images for this book, and to his
colleague, Chris James, Creative and Brand Adviser, for
providing twentieth-century images of The Scout
Association. Many people gave generously of their
knowledge and images, including Mike Donoher, Ken
Johnson, Michael Loomes, Roy Masini, Jeff Robson, Alan
Rodgers, Geoff Stevens, Spelthorne Scouts District
Archive, Colin Walker. A special thank-you goes to Frank
L. Brittain, Archivist for Hertfordshire Scouts, who was so
generous with his time and advice, gave me unlimited cups
of tea and access to the Hertfordshire Scouts Museum and
Archive, and provided many of the images which appear in
the book.

Images are acknowledged as follows: Frank L. Brittain,
Archivist, History & Heritage Support Team,
Hertfordshire Scouts, pages 6, 8 (bottom left and right),
10, 11 (bottom), 13, 16 (bottom), 22 (bottom) 23 (top
and middle), 28 (bottom), 29, 30, 38, 43 (top), 44, 46
(all), 47, 49 (top); Alan Rodgers, page 41 (top);
Spelthorne Scouts District Archive, pages 9 (top) and 21.
All other images courtesy of The Scout Association.

This book helps support The Scout Association, making a
positive difference to the lives of 400,000 young people
across the UK.

Shire Publications is supporting the Woodland Trust, the UK's leading woodland conservation charity, by funding the dedication of trees.

CONTENTS

HOW IT ALL BEGAN

Scouts are known and recognised throughout the world, for the Movement to which they belong is a multicultural, multinational phenomenon. There are some 400,000 young people, including 65,000 girls, between the ages of six and twenty-five in the United Kingdom, and 31 million people participating in Scouting across 216 countries. None of this would have been possible without the foresight, inspiration and initiative of Robert Stephenson Smyth Baden-Powell (B-P), who created the organisation in the early 1900s.

B-P was born in London on 22 February 1857, and throughout his childhood and youth was keenly interested in nature and the great outdoors, camping and hiking. He joined the army at nineteen, and as an officer in the 13th Hussars spent time in India, Africa and Afghanistan honing his tracking and spying skills. Besides becoming an accomplished artist, B-P was an avid reader and writer. By 1899 he had four books in print, with four more published by 1900, including his avant-garde manual of military scouting, *Aids to Scouting*, written to encourage ordinary soldiers to train themselves in reconnaissance skills. But it was the Boer War, and B-P's remarkable actions at the Siege of Mafeking between 4 October 1899 and 16 May 1900, which resulted in him being promoted to major general, and established as a national hero. As H. A. L. Fisher wrote in *A History of Europe*:

> Little perhaps would have been made of the Siege of Mafeking if it had not been defended by a man of genius whose happy resources and light-hearted sallies, telegraphed home while the siege was proceeding, made him a popular favourite with his countrymen.

On his return to Britain in 1903, B-P was appointed Inspector-General of Cavalry, and, despite the demands of the post, spent much of his time thinking about creating a movement for boys. What he had in mind was 'education in high ideals, in self-reliance, in sense of duty, in fortitude, in self-respect, and regard for others – in one word, in those attributes that go to make up

Character.' He also envisaged his scheme appealing to many more than the 54,000 lads in William Smith's popular Boys' Brigade, of which he was a great admirer. With Smith's encouragement he set about writing a book on the lines of *Aids to Scouting*, but this time specifically for boys. B-P said himself, 'here seemed to be the work waiting to my hand for which that damnable notoriety I had incurred could now be usefully employed.' Formulating his strategy consumed much of his spare time, with his developing ideas influenced by Ernest Thompson Seton's Woodcraft Movement and booklet, *The Birch-Bark Roll of the Woodcraft Indians.* But it was an encounter with Sir Arthur Pearson, publisher and founder of Pearson's Fresh Air Fund for Children, which crystallised matters. Drawn together by their mutual interest in the welfare of young people, Pearson was so captivated by B-P's ideas that he immediately agreed to help him make them a reality.

Chief Scout
Sir Robert Baden-
Powell wearing his
Scout uniform and
decorations,
c. 1914.

Part III.   FORTNIGHTLY.   Price 4d. net.

SCOUTING FOR BOYS

BY B-P

LIEUT. GEN.
BADEN POWELL C.B.

PUBLISHED BY HORACE COX, WINDSOR HOUSE, BREAM'S BUILDINGS, LONDON, E

BROWNSEA ISLAND

BADEN-POWELL outlined his initial concept in the pamphlets 'Boy Scouts: A Suggestion' and 'Boy Scouts: Summary of Scheme', but Pearson and B-P agreed not to go further until his ideas had been tried and tested. His experimental camp on Brownsea Island, Dorset, in August 1907, was attended by twenty-two boys, aged between around ten and seventeen years old. The lads were divided up into smaller groups or Patrols, each under responsible charge of a leading boy. For B-P, this system was 'the great step to success.' One Scout, fifteen-year-old Humphrey Noble, recalled in 1957, 'we all had the greatest fun and learnt all about Scoutcraft, tracking, being observant, how to move without being seen and how to make the most of any cover given by the lie of the land.' Percy Everett, Pearson's literary editor, was there for the final campfire, and was equally impressed, as 'the Chief told us thrilling yarns, and himself led the Eengonyama [a Zulu chant] chorus.' He also introduced them to the 'left hand shake', a greeting that has endured as a sign of trust and friendship amongst Scouts.

Buoyed by the success of the Brownsea camp, and as troops were being formed, such as the one at Cottesmore School, Brighton, in November 1907, B-P proceeded with his plans. With Everett's assistance, and working from a tiny office financed by Pearson's generosity, donations from friends and B-P's own slender means, the first serialised edition of his training aid for existing organisations, *Scouting for Boys*, went on sale in local newsagents on 16 January 1908. Five more parts were published at fortnightly intervals before the first complete edition came out on 1 May, and this became the blueprint for the burgeoning Movement. Another weekly publication, *The Scout*, written especially for the boys, was being devised, and the first twenty-page edition appeared on 14 April 1908. For the next fifty-eight years it provided its ever-increasing readership with inspiration, information, adventure stories, news and letters from Scouts. The inaugural great Boy Scout serial, 'The Boys of the Otter Pool', by E. le Breton Martin, appeared in the issue of 6 June 1908, and until his death on 18 January 1941, all but three issues included a yarn written by B-P.

Opposite:
One of the six original parts of *Scouting for Boys*. The complete edition was so successful that it was reprinted four times within a year, and translated into five languages.

The first official Scout camp was held at Humshaugh, Northumberland, in August 1908 and was run very much on the lines of the Brownsea camp. Thirty-six Scouts attended the event, which was presided over by B-P, even though he missed the opening. Patrols and troops were now springing up spontaneously all over the country, including one in Elstree, Hertfordshire, where Percy Everett was persuaded to become Scoutmaster of the 1st Elstree. In Horley, Surrey, two separate groups

B-P at Brownsea Island experimental camp, 1907.

Boys playing at Brownsea Island experimental camp, 1907.

Right: *The Scout* became the longest running weekly publication for boys in the world. The last issue was published in September 1958.

Far right: This June 1908 edition of *The Scout* included instructions on the right way to stop a runaway horse.

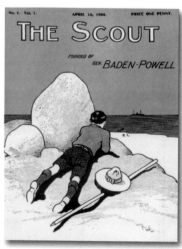

The first picture of 1st Staines and Hythe Scout troop, 1911. This troop was formed in 1909. The location and event are unknown.

were formed, and it took a boxing match between the rivals before their differences were settled and hands shaken. A combined troop, the Horley (B-P), was subsequently formed in 1909, by which time the Brighton area had twelve troops. In the days before purpose-built Scout huts, all sorts of buildings served as meeting places, including an old stable in Elstree, a cottage in Horse-Shoe Lane, Chipping Sodbury, and a cellar under the Methodist Church in Rosehill Street, Conway.

Uniform and equipment were a fundamental part of Scouting, and there was no shortage of guidance on offer in the regular publications. The official

'A Ripping Yarn', c. 1910, and other paintings by Ernest Stafford Carlos (1883–1917), brought the meaning and ethos of Scouting to the attention of a wider audience. Carlos was founder of the 107th London troop.

'wide-awake' brimmed hat, flannel shirt and short trousers with breeches (or a kilt for the Scotsmen) remained relatively unchanged until 1967. In the early years the complete kit, which included haversack, staff, buttonhole badge, shoulder knot and 31-inch-square neckerchief – knotted at the throat and ends – cost around eight shillings. Some troops included the cost of uniform in the subscription, an amount which varied from troop to troop. By the end of 1908 there were at least 50,000 Scouts, and the Movement had spread to Ireland, Australia, Canada, New Zealand and South Africa. As Percy Everett proudly remarked, this was 'certainly the biggest development of any youth movement in the world in its first year of existence.'

Scouts were introduced to specific aspects of the Movement through B-P's inspirational Camp Fire Yarns in *The Scout*. The second described the

Right, far right and below: The scouting magazines carried advertisements for everything that a Scout or Scouter could possibly need.

Scout Law and the Scout Oath, which became the Scout Promise in 1912.

> On my honour I promise that:
> 1) I will do my duty to God, and the King;
> 2) I will do my best to help others, whatever it costs me;
> 3) I know the Scout Law and will obey it.

Later, the Promise was adjusted to accommodate Scouts of a variety of faiths.

The third yarn was all about tests and the badge system, for as far as B-P was concerned, this was the best way of encouraging boys to keep improving themselves and move upwards from Second Class to First Class Scout. Strict rules applied to the wearing of badges, and B-P instructed that 'All medals and badges are only worn as above when Scouts are on duty or in camp. At other times they should be worn on the right breast of the waistcoat, underneath the jacket.' The award of a 'Wolf' badge was quite exceptional, denoting a very special distinction, and entitled the holder to 'make the sign with the first finger and thumb opened out, the remaining fingers clenched, thumb upwards.' A Patrol Leader could be elevated to Silver Wolf a year later by earning just twenty-four proficiency test badges, but this award became much harder to acquire from January 1912.

These khaki felt proficiency badges are twelve of the thirty-three that Scouts could aim for by 1909, the most popular being the Ambulance and Cyclist badges. These are, clockwise from top left: Farmer; Fire Fighter/Fireman; Electrician; Debator.

An early membership card, showing St George, the patron saint of all Scouts.

NAME . . . .

You are now a Scout.
So, Sleeves up — and tackle your job !

Robert Baden Powell
Chief Scout

11

THE BOY SCOUTS

AUGUST, 1911.

(BADEN-POWELL'S)

HEADQUARTERS GAZETTE

Contents

No. 2.   AUGUST, 1911.   Vol. 5.

Price TWOPENCE.

Published by

THE BOY SCOUTS' HEADQUARTERS,

116 Victoria Street, London. S.W.

Editor—Mr. H. GEOFFREY ELWES.

BE PREPARED

NEW ADVANCES

THE YEAR 1909 was full of new advances: the opening of the Scout Headquarters in rented accommodation in Victoria Street, London, and the appointment of the first Scout County Commissioners (CC), personal representatives of the Chief Scout in various districts. Percy Everett, as CC for Hertfordshire, was cited as a model for others to follow. The announcement in *The Scout* on 5 June 1909, of the copyright-registered 'fleur de lis' World Badge, was a momentous occasion. B-P explained: '[it] shows the north of a map, on a map or a compass. It is the badge of the Scout in the army because he shows the way; so, too, a peace Scout shows the way in doing his duty and helping others.'

A new monthly paper, the *Headquarters (HQ) Gazette*, replaced the single page in *The Scout* in July, and was written specifically to keep Scout officials, at home and across the Empire, up-to-date with information. Yet another 'first' that year was the introduction of the 'King's Scout', an accolade which King Edward VII agreed, at B-P's suggestion, could be awarded to First Class Scouts who had passed a total of fourteen special tests for efficiency. Within weeks of the qualifying criteria appearing in the *HQ Gazette*, Patrol Leader Victor Watkins, of the Broadstone Scout troop in Poole, Dorset, was encouraged by his Scoutmaster to hurry and get the last badge he needed. On 10 December 1909, he became the first ever King's Scout, proudly wearing his royal crown badge. B-P was equally delighted to be made a Knight Commander of the Royal Victorian Order in recognition of his services to the country, and for founding the Boy Scouts.

The first National Scout Rally at the Crystal Palace on 4 September attracted a phenomenal 11,000 Scouts, and one young lad, Walter Stemp, of the 1st Ewhurst, recalled that the regimental band of The Queen's Royal West Surrey Regiment was in attendance. So were a group of Girl Scouts in makeshift Scout uniform who wanted to be part of the Movement, and it was B-P's recognition of this upsurge of female interest that led to the establishment of the Girl Guide Association in 1910, with his sister Agnes at the helm.

Opposite:
The *HQ Gazette*,
August 1911.

Above: An early Arrowhead badge. The two stars and ten points represent the original ten Scout laws.

DIEU ET MON DROIT

AS A KING'S SCOUT you have prepared yourself for service to God and your fellow-men, and have shown yourself a worthy member of the great SCOUT BROTHERHOOD. I wish you God speed on your journey through life; may it prove for you a joyous adventure. *George R.*

Above right: King's Scout Certificate. The badge was worn on the left arm above the First Class badge, surrounded by the qualifying badges.

This was a turning point for B-P. The first UK Scout Census in August 1910 showed that there were 100,298 Scouts, 7,688 Scouters (adult leaders) and that 1,632 King's Scout Badges had been issued. Besides this there was rapid worldwide expansion of Scouting, and in 1908 alone, Scouting began in Australia, Canada, Ireland, Malta, New Zealand and South Africa. Combining soldiering with Scouting had become increasingly difficult for him, and after great consideration he decided to concentrate on his new Movement. With the King's approval, he resigned from the army, retiring officially on 7 May 1910, just one day after the monarch's death. Royal patronage continued with King George V, and not only were there Boy Scouts on duty at the Coronation on 22 June 1911, but some 35,000 lads from home and abroad attended the King's Rally at Windsor Great Park on 4 July. 1st Ashwell Patrol Leader Harry Bonnett's abiding memory was of having the most amazing day of his life, despite the endless pre-rally drill practice and the exhausting journey. Scouting was becoming so successful that it spawned, amongst other items, a host of board games and toys, many of them approved by the Association.

B-P inspecting Boy Scouts at the Crystal Palace Rally, 4 September 1909.

Nowhere was the royal connection more significant than in the signing of the Royal Charter of Incorporation on 4 January 1912, marking King George V's official recognition of the Scouting Movement and of B-P's role as leader. B-P's marriage to Olave St Clair Soames on 30 October, just four weeks after they had both attended the first ever Hampshire County Rally on Southampton Common and inspected 2,700 Scouts, was yet another cause for celebration.

Above: Besides board and card games, there were jigsaw puzzles, printing sets, tin toys, postcards and cigarette cards, all of which have become highly collectable memorabilia.

Middle: B-P and his wife, Olave St Clair Soames, by the 20hp six-cylinder Standard Laundulet car, given to them as a wedding present by the Scouts. It was paid for by subscribers, including £411 14s 1d from Scout troops, and was presented on 13 May 1913 by the Duke of Connaught.

Bottom: Thousands of troops at the King's Rally in Windsor Great Park, with banners, bugles, drums and drumsticks whirling. 4 July 1911.

Warington B-P's book laid down the rules, regulations, badges, ranks and uniform requirements for the Sea Scouts, along with advice on training. He said, 'Sea Scouting is simply a brand of boy Scouting.'

NEW BRANCHES ARE FORMED

The majority of Scouts kept their feet on terra firma, but B-P was already directing boys towards the water with his instructions in *Scouting for Boys*: 'A Scout should be able to manage a boat, to bring it properly alongside a ship or pier', and the Seaman Badge was one of the first five efficiency badges to be introduced *c.* December 1908. There were early signs of a Sea Scouting branch developing in Glasgow, as reported in *The Scout* in February 1909, followed by the introduction of a Seamanship proficiency badge in June. Water-based events formed part of B-P's third camp in August 1909, on the training ship *Mercury* at Buckler's Hard on the Beaulieu River, and by October of that year Sea Scouting was acknowledged as a separate branch, with its own policy and an authorised special uniform. Even before B-P's six-penny booklet, *Sea Scouting for Boys*, was published in May 1911, he had obtained permission from the Admiralty for Sea Scouts to be established as Seamen and Coast Watchers. But it was his brother Warington's 1912 publication, *Sea Scouting and Seamanship for Boys*, written at B-P's request, that became the first official handbook. The great Leysdown (Isle of Sheppey) tragedy in August 1912, when nine Scouts drowned as their cutter capsized, could have been

A postcard image of the stricken vessel and of the people who rescued the Boy Scouts at Leysdown in 1912.

the end of Sea Scouting, but this, and other disasters, failed to deter them. The *HQ Gazette* did announce, in early 1914, that 'No boat training shall be undertaken unless the Scout can swim fifty yards', and another handbook, *Seamanship for Scouts*, by Lieutenant Commander W. H. Stuart Garnett, which appeared in August 1914, laid much greater emphasis upon safety management.

SOMETHING FOR THE YOUNGER BOYS?

It was not long before boys under Scout age were clamouring to join their older brothers, but B-P was concerned that a flood of small boys, already appearing in some groups, would have the effect of making Scouting a 'kid's game'. Seeking a solution, Everett was asked to prepare a draft scheme, and by early 1914, following careful consideration and various alterations at HQ, agreement was reached for Wolf Cub packs, to be run on an experimental basis. The eight to twelve year olds had their own uniform, a Law and a Promise suited to their level of understanding, and progressive First and Second Star tests like the bigger boys. But instead of being explorers, pioneers or 'peace Scouts', B-P gave the youngsters their own romantic background of the jungle, basing the scheme on the *Jungle Book*, written by his friend, Rudyard Kipling. Miss Vera Barclay was already a pioneering female Scouter when she introduced the 1st Hertford Heath Cub Pack to her troop in January 1915, so becoming one of the first Wolf Cub Akelas, named after one of Kipling's characters. By 1916, Barclay was National Wolf Cub Secretary. The pressures of wartime delayed planning, and it was not until December 1916 that Wolf Cubs were officially launched at Caxton Hall, London, and *The Wolf Cub's Handbook*, written by B-P with Vera Barclay's inspirational ideas and assistance, was published.

The Definitive Edition of the *Wolf Cub's Handbook* was published in 1980 as the 17th edition. B-P was keen to 'bring boys under Scout discipline at an earlier and more receptive age.'

These Wolf Cubs, practising semaphore, are wearing their special uniform of a green jersey, knotted pack scarf, shorts, long socks and a green school-type cap with yellow piping, c. 1916.

THE FIRST WORLD WAR

'To the boys of Britain. Come and join the nearest troops in your district and do your duty like a man.'

B-P's message, August 1914.

B-P was quick to respond to the looming crisis of war on the home front and circulated to every County Commissioner asking for all Scouts to be mobilised and ready to be of service in whatever capacity was needed. Just three days after Britain declared war on Germany on 4 August 1914, the Admiralty asked for 1,000 Sea Scouts to do coast watching on the East Coast, and during the course of the war more than 20,000 Scouts undertook this important role. Their duties included patrolling the beaches, salvaging wreckage and watching out for fishing boats that worked unauthorised hours at night. The lads had to examine all boats that came into shore and check that permits were in order, and were required to answer all naval calls on the telephone and report vessels passing up and down. Boys from the 32nd Renfrew & Inverclyde formed part of a coastguard duty on submarine watch during the first year of the war (others from the same troop volunteered to become ward orderlies at Greenock War Hospital, Smithston).

On land, and within days of war being declared, Percy Everett, who led the way in establishing the Home Front Scout organisation, had promised his Chief Constable the services of 1,000 of his 1,300 Scouts. Before long the Hertfordshire lads were undertaking all manner of jobs, from whitewashing various things for the military, to making sandbags and even providing an escort for a lunatic. By July 1915, the *Penny Pictorial Magazine* was informing readers that 50,000 Scouts were directly or indirectly engaged in war work. They gave examples of Scouts sitting in hospitals writing letters for soldiers who could not do so themselves, and of hundreds of boys being employed by the Soldiers' and Sailors' Homes Association, ensuring that money, clothing and food reached the homes where they were needed. Meanwhile, on 25 July 1915, 'eight Scouts (of the 4th St Albans) were down at the railway station all night, helping to serve tea and cakes to the soldiers who were going to the Dardanelles.' They also had to

Opposite:
Scouts harvesting flax on a farm during the First World War.

Sea Scouts having dinner after coast watching duties during the First World War.

Sea Scouts firing a rocket signal to warn lifeboat crew of a vessel in distress, 1914.

Boys of the
1st Staines and
Hythe Troop
collecting waste
paper for the war
effort, c.1916.

turn round signposts to confuse any German soldier who might land, a stark reminder for these young boys of the reality of war. Collecting eggs to serve as a little luxury for wounded soldiers became a popular pursuit across the country, and in the Trowbridge section the boys were known to have tramped ten miles or more in the space of one week, amassing no fewer than 2,000 eggs. Nor were those fighting the war on foreign soil forgotten, as Scouts held book collections and sent parcels out to soldiers all over the world, with 700 sent from Greenock alone. Troops in France also benefited from funds raised at home by the Cubs and Scouts, for some of the money went towards the YMCA/British Scout Huts.

Scout buglers found themselves in demand: besides sounding the 'All Clear' after air raids, they were also attached to local police stations. Stanley Bird was kept on by G Division in Kings Cross, London, and had to travel in an ambulance after an air raid, repeatedly blowing two notes on his bugle as a warning of the emergency. The efforts of the Scout bugler in St Albans prompted Mr Part, a pillar of the community, to launch a 'khaki capes' fund for the local troop. These were worn only when a Scout was in uniform and on duty, and had to be returned in good condition with the details of the loan entered into a log book. B-P's specially instituted War Service Badges for boys over fourteen carrying out approved 'war work' became the goal of many. F. Bees and M. Harford of the 1st Chipping Sodbury earned theirs in late 1916 by volunteering for twenty-eight consecutive days at Horton Red Cross Hospital. In the first year of the war alone, over 20,000 such badges were awarded, with Hertfordshire Scouts earning 996 badges during the

The Scout/YMCA Hut at Étaples, officially opened by B-P on 1 January 1916, was the biggest of all the Huts. It cost about £1,000 and could house 1,000 men, providing troops behind the front lines with shelter, food and entertainment, c. 1916–18.

course of the war, as well as three of the thirty-five Silver Crosses awarded for gallantry in the British Empire. Added to these achievements, boys from the St Albans Scouts took on acting roles in the nationally screened, 1917 Trans Atlantic Studios film, *Boy Scouts, Be Prepared.*

There were many Scouts who lost their lives in the conflict, including six of the original Brownsea Island boys. Most outstanding was sixteen-year-old John ('Jack') Cornwell of the St Mary's Mission (Manor Park) troop, a Royal Navy sight-setter on one of HMS *Chester*'s 5.5-inch gun crews, who was mortally wounded at the Battle of Jutland. The cruiser was shelled by German guns in May 1916, but despite being mortally injured he stayed at his post to the bitter end, surrounded by dead and wounded colleagues, awaiting orders. He died days later after being brought ashore at Grimsby. Posthumously, he was awarded the Victoria Cross, the youngest person in the First World War to be so honoured, and B-P granted him the Bronze Cross, the highest medal for heroism at the time. But most enduring was the institution, in September 1916, of the 'Cornwell Badge', officially described as 'an exceptional award in respect of pre-eminently high character and devotion to duty, together with great courage, endurance or gallantry.' The first Scout to

This picture of bugler George Foxlee, of the 4th St Albans troop, appeared on the front page of *The Times*, and other papers in 1915–16, under the heading 'All Clear'.

One of the shots for the film *Boy Scouts be Prepared*, including Charles Dymoke Green, District Commissioner of St Albans (far left); B-P pointing his cane; and Percy Everett, County Commissioner (far right).

THE GREAT BOY SCOUT.

receive the badge was Patrol Leader Shepherd in November 1916. Boy Scout memorials served as public reminders of lost lives, but in 1921 the 1st Downend, South Gloucestershire, could claim to be the only troop in the country to have one built on public land.

On 30 September 1916, proclaimed as 'John Cornwell Day', every school was sent a picture of Cornwell, and seven million schoolchildren bought a commemorative stamp. The money raised helped fund a ward in Queen Mary's Star and Garter Home for war-disabled soldiers and sailors.

An ambulance paid for by Scouts, through fundraising during the First World War.

Rovering to Success

A book of Life-sport
for young men by
Sir Robert Baden Powell Bt.
With sixty illustrations
by the author

FOR
SUMMARY
OF THIS BOOK
SEE
BACK OF

THE 1920s

'ONE FELT AT THE TIME that the shackles which had held us in bondage during the weary war years had suddenly been cast off.'

F. Haydn Dimmock, *Bare Knee Days*.

By the time the Armistice was signed on 11 November 1918, Scout HQ had moved to their own premises in Buckingham Palace Road, London, and the calls, especially from young heroes returning from the Great War, for the establishment of a section for older boys with the objectives and activities tailored to suit the age group, had been answered. A scheme for senior Scouts was introduced in May 1917, and renamed Rover Scouts the following August. Aimed at those over seventeen-and-a-half years old, B-P described this as 'the third progressive step in the education of the Boy Scout'. 'Brotherhood and Service' became the Rover Motto and was announced in a 1918 pamphlet, 'Rules for Rovers'; the section was firmly established by November 1919.

Besides this, the Movement continued to grow in various directions. Abroad, over seventy countries had started Scouting in the decade after 1907, whilst at home, the donation of the 55-acre Gilwell Park estate, near Chingford, Essex, for use as a camping ground, gave B-P the ideal location and opportunity for training Scout Officers, as they were known. Within weeks of Gilwell Park opening in July 1919, nineteen men wearing shorts, knee socks and rolled-up shirt sleeves were attending B-P's personally designed inaugural Wood Badge training camp, and his book, *Aids to Scoutmastership*, became their bible. In recognition of having completed the course, each was given a Wood Badge: two small wooden beads on a piece of leather thong, adapted from a Zulu chief's necklace which B-P had acquired during the Mafeking campaign. As a way of celebrating the end of the war, and bringing the youth of the world together, B-P instigated plans to hold the very first international gathering of Scouts at Olympia, London, in the summer of 1920. Unlike any that followed, this was held indoors, and the great arena had to be covered with twelve inches of earth and turf to enable tents to be pitched. Between 30 July and 7 August

Opposite:
Subtitled
'A Guide for Young
Manhood', B-P's
book, *Rovering to
Success*, was
published in 1922.
Rovers had their
own lexicon, with
those waiting to
be initiated into
a Rover Crew
known as 'Rover
Squires'.

Right: A Rover Mate, with his Rover shoulder strap and shoulder knot, and Rover Mate's Red Stripes on his shirt pocket, c. 1918.

Centre:
1st Gilwell Park Wood Badge Course, 1919, with B-P seated centre front row.

Bottom: The White House, Gilwell Park, July 1919. The grounds were so overgrown that regular parties of Scouts spent their weekends clearing the estate. The old house was in a dilapidated state and needed major restoration, costing far more than was originally estimated.

P.L.'s Hat Badge (top only)
R.S. Badge on Strap.
Hat Cord behind head
Rambler's Badge
Rover Shoulder Strap.
Rolled Sleeves.
Service Stars.
Knot in Scarf.
Rover Shoulder Knot
Thumbstick
Scout Badge (cloth).
Rover Mate's Red Stripes.
Skean Dhu (optional).
Red Garter Tabs
Rover Mate

over 8,000 Scouts from around the world attended the conference and so-called Jamboree – a new word in the Scout lexicon – and participated in a vast range of activities from handicrafts and models, to camp pitching, competitions and community singing. The culmination of this great event was the acclamation of B-P as Chief Scout of the World.

The Jamboree was soon followed by a unique opportunity for one Senior Scout, aged between seventeen and nineteen, to join the Antarctic explorer, Sir Ernest Shackleton, as a crewmember aboard the *Quest*, on his trip to the Pole in July 1921. An astonishing 1,700 boys from across the country applied, and Shackleton ultimately chose two boys from B-P's shortlist of ten: Patrol Leaders James Marr, 1st Aberdeen, and Norman Mooney of the 2nd Orkney. The pair were full members of the small eighteen-man crew, and Marr, working as a deckhand, kept a log of his trip, published as *Into the Frozen South* in 1922. His entry for 28 December 1921 serves as a reminder that this was a hazardous journey:

Sir Ernest Shackleton and Percy Everett, on the roof of Scout HQ in September 1921, with eight of the ten finalist Scouts. Patrol Leader James Marr is far right, in his kilt; Patrol Leader Norman Mooney is behind him.

> I came on watch at two in the morning. We were running before a strong gale and pitching and rolling heavily. The waves were quite thirty feet in height, and were breaking over the aft end of the ship and on the bridge. I was looking out on the bridge when the officer of the watch sent me down for a tin of milk. Crossing the foot-bridge I was washed right off my feet. I hung onto a ledge with my hands and so was saved from further disaster. By seven in the morning the waves were averaging between thirty and forty feet high. Many were over forty feet. The gale had increased to a hurricane.

Mooney succumbed to sea sickness and was forced to leave the *Quest* at Madeira, and Shackleton died of a heart attack on 5 January 1922, aged only forty-eight, the day after the vessel reached South Georgia.

The *Daily Mail* also ran a competition, independent of the trip, inviting Scouts and Sea Scouts to write a 250-word essay entitled 'Why I'd like to go with Shackleton'. Twelve-year-old Frank Sears of the 3rd Boxmoor was one of the successful applicants who won an all-expenses-paid trip to visit London and the *Quest* prior to its departure. With £1 pocket money he travelled on a train for the first time in his life, had a bus tour of the capital, were taken to a West End show, and experienced the novelty of sleeping in a hammock overnight, including falling out of the other side as he tried to get in.

B-P blowing the famous kudu horn in 1919. The kudu is a species of African antelope. The original horn is now at Gilwell Park.

Around this time, the problem of creased neckerchiefs, or scarves, was resolved with the creation of the 'woggle' by Bill Shankley, an eighteen-year-old campsite employee at Gilwell Park, in the 1920s. The British ring, through which the scarf was threaded, was a version of the American 'Boon Doggle', and was made of fine leather strips plaited in a knot. It was officially approved for general use by the committee of the Scout Movement Council in July 1923.

Up and down the country, conferences, county camps and rallies were held, there were county cycle marathons, and football teams were formed. In January 1923 the first edition of *The Scouter,* a monthly magazine for Leaders, was published, and in September 1924 the first Scout Musical Festival was held at the Royal College of Music. The Special Tests Branch was introduced the following year, becoming the Handicapped Scouts Branch in 1936. When the inaugural National Rover Moot – gathering of Rover Scouts – was held at the Royal Albert Hall, London in April 1926, the lads put on a

The Scouter was created by amalgamating the *HQ Gazette* and *The Trail*, the magazine of the Scout County of London, under a new name.

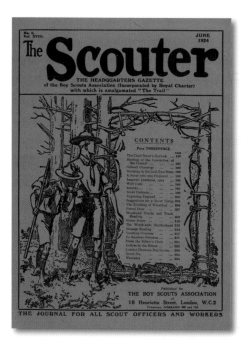

theatrical review based completely on the legends of King Arthur and the Knights of the Round Table, the same tales that B-P used to inspire the Rover Rituals. The year 1928 saw the formation of a new branch of Sea Scouting – Deep Sea Scouts – enabling young men who wanted to begin their working life at sea to continue as Scouts. When the Scout Movement came of age in July 1929, 30,000 Scouts representing seventy-nine countries joined the celebration at the third World Jamboree, held in Arrowe Park, Birkenhead. Seeing and hearing B-P open the proceedings by blowing the famous kudu horn (the Matabele war horn first used by him to summon the Scouts at the Brownsea camp) and saluting him as the newly appointed Lord Baden-Powell of Gilwell was an awesome experience. But the Bishop of Birkenhead's abiding 'Scout' memory was of the mud, which he thought would probably cling to him until his dying day.

THE 1930s

THE MOVEMENT went from strength to strength: it had a total international membership of 2,039,349 in 1931, and continued to offer boys the chance to develop all manner of skills, including musical ones. The *Hackney Scout Song Book*, a mix of folk and popular songs, first published in 1921, had become so popular that it was widely distributed to troops outside the local borough. Many troops had bugle, fife and drum marching bands, and, like the 1st Eynsham, played at village carnivals and fêtes, and at local football cup matches, as well as holding an annual concert that toured the neighbouring villages. But it was the advent of the Gang Shows that gave boys the chance to really shine. When actor-producer Ralph Reader, a Rover Scout himself, was asked to put on a 'concert' to raise funds for a swimming-pool at the Scout's Downe campsite, he never imagined that the London variety show he produced, for which he wrote the lyrics and music, would become an enduring tradition within the Scout Movement, and be adopted all over the world. The first-ever review, 'The Gang's All Here!', attributed to an anonymous 'Holborn Rover', was staged at the Scala Theatre in London between 30 October and 1 November 1932, and had a cast

Advertisements for equipment and other items in *The Scouter*, January 1932.

The Gang's All Here 1932.

OPENING

This special issue of "These Are The Times" celebrates sixty glorious years of Gang Show and commemorates its Founder, Ralph Reader, who died 10 years ago. How pleased he would be to see his creation flourishing and the spirit of Gang Show thriving.

It is full of personal memories of the Man and His Show. It traces the development of the Show from its beginnings in 1932 until today and hints at the future.

The Scout Show started in 1932 and although the 1939 Show was written and rehearsed it was never staged, Scout uniform being changed for RAF uniform. The London Scout Gang Show returned in 1950 and ran until 1974, Scout Shows in the rest of the country have continued since then and 'our Movement' within the Movement is stronger than ever. How proud that Man would be.

There is mention in our pages of the Royal Command Performances, the Gang Show film and Boy Scout. But there were also other productions 'Happy Families' and its sequel 'Next Door', 'The Voyager of the Venturer' plus many more. Ralph was featured in 'This Is Your Life' and made many other television appearances. His name was synonomous with Albert Hall productions. One story he used to tell was about the young Scout who asked how many productions he had staged at the Albert Hall - "100" came the answer, "Oh is that one every year" - "No _son I missed a couple". How typical of Ralph - great humour and warmth, always able to top everything.

'These are the times" - they really were, are and will be.

Compiled by Mary   *Design & Layout: Rue*   *Editor: David Clay*

'The Gang's All Here', 1932.

of 150. The costumes were borrowed, the scenery hired and even though it was not a sell-out, the show raised £150, and, more importantly, was rapturously received. B-P quickly persuaded Reader to put on another show the next year, which again played to packed houses. Before long, Gang Shows began to spring up around the country, from St Albans to Stoke, and Newcastle to Crewe, where their first show, 'Flying High', went on stage at the old Town Hall in 1938. St Albans District followed in 1939, in the presence of Reader himself. Only active Scout members could take part, and once admitted to full Gang Show status – only given to shows of the very highest standard – the cast were entitled to wear the duplicated 'Red Neckerchief' with its distinctive Gang Show emblem. Corby got their emblem in 1962, just four years after putting on their first show, and Christchurch were awarded theirs by Ralph Reader himself at the local Pontins ballroom in November 1966.

Scouts were regularly 'on the ground' at royal events, and the Coronation of King George VI on 12 May 1937 was no exception. 125 Rover Scouts were on duty outside Westminster Abbey; others sold souvenir programmes whilst many more helped the police erect, man and dismantle 2,400 crash barriers along the route. The Gang Show was already set to reach a much wider audience with the premiere of the Pinewood Studios film at the Lyceum Theatre, London, in April, but the greatest accolade came in November 1937, when it became the first ever amateur production to appear at a Royal Command performance. Ten-year-old Dick Rundle was one of two Cub Scouts picked to play 'The Boy' in the

Coronation scene, but regulations prevented him performing for two consecutive weeks. Nor could he appear in the second half, as it was deemed 'too late for such youthful innocents.'

Amid such joyful events, war was on the horizon, and in a prescient move, B-P wrote to the Home Secretary in 1937, offering the services of Scouts and Rover Scouts in connection with Air Raid Precautions. It was not long before Scouts were being encouraged to qualify for Ambulance, Pathfinder and Signaller badges. Even as the country was bracing itself for war, the Scouts were trying out new ideas, and in the summer of 1939 the inaugural Scouts' National Soap Box Derby was held. The speedsters were made from a soap box mounted on a plank, with two wheels back and front, and required a degree of ingenuity in the construction. The 58th Birmingham troop built the steering mechanism for theirs by sandwiching ball bearings between two frying pans. When the finals were held on 1 July 1939, a 5-mile-long stream of cars moved at a snail's pace from Esher to Brooklands race track; apart from the 5,000 Scouts, between 30,000 and 40,000 people turned up for the event, and saw Sir Malcolm Campbell, the famous speedman, award the prizes. The outbreak of the Second World War brought these races to an end, and the London Gang Shows came to a halt too, as Reader joined the RAF and was sent to France with the British Expeditionary Force.

The British Racing Drivers Club arranged for the two semi-finals of the Scouts' National Soap Box Derby to be held on recognised race tracks at the Crystal Palace and Donington Park during scheduled race meetings, where these scouts were competing in 1939.

THE SECOND
WORLD WAR

Wartime inevitably had an impact on the Movement as many Scouters and Rover Scouts disappeared into the Forces. Besides this, Gilwell Park was requisitioned by the Army, which impacted on Wood Badge training camps. Many troops found themselves leaderless, leaving willing but untrained teenage Scouts in charge, including the Norcott & Kentwood in Berkshire; they were unexpectedly rescued, however, by a scientist working at the British Museum, who knocked on the door of the Methodist church hall one evening and 'came in through the blackout curtain asking if he could help.' And help he did, leading the troop into a brilliant period of Scouting. The blackout meant that meeting times and venues often had to be changed, but many troops found it difficult to arrange daytime weekend meetings. London and the provincial cities were particularly badly affected, but the Holborn troop came up with a novel scheme, 'Lone Scouting in London', and issued a monthly circular to members who were still in the capital, and who spent many of their leisure hours in public shelters. A shortage of clothing, exacerbated by clothes rationing, also presented a problem, prompting a good market in second-hand clothing, and there were fears, largely unfounded, that boys would defect to the Air Training Corps and Cadet Corps, who offered free uniforms.

Despite the war, camps continued to be held wherever possible – never within ten miles of the coast – but the basic rules had to be adjusted, and it became essential to camp under trees, often in chalk pits, using the bushes for cover. A Liverpool troop, sent to Kershopefoot on the English/Scottish border in the summer of 1941 to help the Forestry Commission, were disconcerted to find they had to pitch their tents in a field without a tree in sight. Campfires had to be extinguished in time for the blackout, and pristine white patrol tents, all too obvious from the sky, were painted in camouflage colours. With no other

The War Service Armband was worn by Scouts when they were doing tasks in support of the war effort.

transport available Patrol Leaders had to use their initiative to move heavy camping gear around, even converting a pram into a trailer for the back of a bicycle. In the early days of the war spirits were high, and recreating scenes from wartime was a popular activity. On one occasion members of the 85th Renfrew and Inverclyde troop, camping at Everton, had three boys pretend to be escaped German prisoners of war on the run. The rest of the troop hunted them out, which they did with much hilarity, belying the seriousness of the situation.

Scouts were well and truly ready to lend a hand during the Second World War, and did so in a vast array of ways. Between 1 and 3 September 1939, the 3rd Boxmoor, Hertfordshire troop found themselves helping to receive about 5,000 London mothers, children and infants in arms, with 847 evacuees arriving on one train alone. The task was enormous and

A Scout helping with the evacuation of children from London, c. 1939.

varied, and included carrying a small child or luggage, providing drinking water, or forming a human fence along the edge of the platform to prevent any toddler falling over. Elsewhere, boys were sent to help at the dispersal centres, often located at the Town Hall. There were plenty of Scouts who helped out at first-aid posts, and very often they found themselves being used as 'casualties' to enable Red Cross volunteers to hone the first aid procedures in the event of an emergency. On Teeside it was decided that the Boy Scouts should patrol the shore at night to report any activity at sea, although Alan Gordon, who belonged to a local troop, wondered what on earth they could or would have done if they had seen anything. For the Sea Scouts, life became a mix of adventure and danger, especially for the 1st Mortlake Sea Scouts, who helped with the evacuation of Dunkirk in

Scouts on bicycles awaiting messages from the Air Raid Precautions telephone exchange, c. 1939.

May 1940, running the gauntlet of enemy fire in their motor picket-boat, *Minotaur*. Other Sea Scout troops assisted with firefighting both during and after the Blitz on London.

Dennis Snell, a 15-year-old Scout in Hereford, volunteered to become a bicycle messenger, and was issued with a black painted steel helmet with a large white 'M' at the front. Blackout rules extended to bicycle lights, so the top half of the lamp was painted black. Uniformed Scouts were also required to carry an axe, which was to be used to smash the back wheels of the bicycle to disable it if an invasion took place. Providing emergency communications was a real challenge, but was resolved in Reading, Berkshire, by having a field telephone van on standby. This was not for the faint hearted, for one Scout had to climb a ladder balanced on the roof of the vehicle and then try and tie telephone cables high up on streetlight poles. Scouters working in the front line at home, especially during the Blitz, regularly risked their lives in the line of duty. Some, like Patrol Leader George Collins, a Sea Scout of the 12th Shoreditch (Jubilee), who rescued three children from a house in Barnet, Hertfordshire during an air raid on 8 October 1940, survived, and he was awarded the Silver Cross for bravery. But seventeen-year-old Frank Davis of the 11th Bermondsey & Rotherhithe (St James), on duty as an Air Raid Warden on 8 December 1940, was not so lucky. Having rescued a fellow Scout messenger, he was killed by enemy action, and was posthumously awarded the Bronze Cross for conspicuous bravery and devotion to duty. Other boys, like London Scout Jim Wilcox, became involved with the local fire-watching team, and he recalled spending time 'on rooftops with a stirrup pump and a bucket of water looking out for fires' during the Blitz.

A fund for war-distressed Scouts had already been established in 1940, but other fundraising activities became commonplace. Kenley Scouts, for one, produced and sold cards with drawings and watercolours of aircraft as a way of raising money for the Spitfire Fund and the Malta Relief Fund. Community activities included collecting waste paper, which, in July 1940 Hertford District Scouts did 'satisfactorily', managing to sell one load weighing more than 13 hundredweight to a local fishmonger. The important thing was that not only was the quantity of paper recorded, but the time spent collecting was noted, for after one hundred hours a boy qualified for the Scouts National Service Badge. Later in the war, Scouts in Wallington dispensed with the horse-drawn van, and manned the council dust-carts during organised 'salvage weeks' to make large, well-publicised summer evening collections. Meanwhile, across the country, scouts were busy picking fruit for jam making, gathering rose hips, collecting tons of horse chestnuts – without the husks – for medicinal purposes, and helping local farmers with the harvest. Mr Ashmole of Nell Bridge Farm was so pleased with the work done by his local troop, the 1st Adderbury, that he rewarded them with the gift of a first-aid box.

In the midst of all this Scout activity, the Movement mourned the death of B-P on 8 January 1941, but the appointments two months later of Lord Somers as Chief Scout of the British Empire and Percy Everett as Deputy Chief Scout for Britain ensured that the Movement was in safe hands.

War work offered Cubs and Scouts an unprecedented opportunity of earning their National Service Badge and of acquiring new skills, no more so than when the green light was given to the formation of Air Scout troops in late January 1941. There had been repeated calls for a separate branch devoted to aviation since the start of the First World War, but despite initiatives to promote 'air mindedness', and the introduction of gliding as a Scout activity in the interwar years, it was the Battle of Britain and the shortage of pilots that provided the impetus for the Air Scouts, with their distinctive beret and blue shorts. 5th Rushden Air Scouts were the first of their kind in Northamptonshire and were unique at the time in having their own aircraft, the gift of a gentleman from Wilby, which was kept in a paddock off Washbrook Road. Following the first national Air Scout Camp held in summer 1942, over 10,000 people attended the Air Scout Exhibition held in London in December that year. A more unusual

Scouts collecting recycling on their trek cart, c. 1940. By the close of 1940, Scouts had collected 35,000 tons of waste paper.

activity involving flight was the training of carrier pigeons, which John Dick of 45th Renfrewshire became involved with. The birds were a very important form of communication, and John and his fellow Scouts were regularly called upon to help train them by moving them from point A to point B.

Despite the enormous amount of war work being undertaken by the Scouts, wider society remained largely ignorant of their efforts, so in 1941 the Association commissioned a booklet, *They Were Prepared*, and produced a film, *Men of Tomorrow*, in the largely unrealised hope of raising public awareness. Certainly, most people remained completely unaware of the role played by the Scouts International Relief Service (SIRS) whose members, male and female adult Scout Leaders, went abroad on humanitarian missions. The first left for Greece in March 1944, and involved delivering 1,000 tons of food and 50,000 articles of clothing to families and prisoners of war. Other such expeditions followed, but the most challenging came a year later, when ten SIRS teams were called upon to help other organisations, including the International Red Cross, at the recently relieved Belsen concentration camp. One team, No.102, was selected to help the sixty-odd surviving children, whose only obvious sign of life, was 'large eyes in the little emaciated faces.' These were horrors that none of the SIRS team ever forgot. By then some 13,000 visitors had enjoyed the first national Sea Scout Exhibition, held at the London Scottish Drill Hall in April 1944, and Gilwell Park, which had been requisitioned during the war, was about to be returned to the Movement, paving the way for a new era in Scouting history.

Air Scouts from St Paul's School, in the grounds of their evacuated school at Easthampstead Park, watching one of their group drawing a picture of a Spitfire, c. 1940s.

The SCOUTER

Jubilee   Number

July 1957   1907   1957   9d

INTO THE POST-WAR ERA

THE SECOND WORLD WAR had a severe impact on numbers in the Scout Movement, especially within the Rover Scout section, for countless lads had been 'called up', and many of them lost their lives. National membership slumped from 38,000 before the war to around 7,290 in 1945, and following the publication in September 1945 of *The Road Ahead*, a national review commissioned in April 1941, the decision was reached, in 1946, to introduce a Senior Scout Section. The so-called 'Austerity Olympics', held in the summer of 1948, gave Scouts a wonderful chance to show off their skills. The British Olympic Committee readily accepted the offer of Scout volunteers, with one admirer describing them as 'the oil of the Olympic wheels.' Max Poultney was fifteen years old, and belonged to a Scout troop in North Harrow, Middlesex, and was chosen to carry the country banner for Belgium at the opening ceremony:

> We were all given a lunch pack containing food and drink. It was a very hot day and I distinctly remember wandering around outside the Wembley Stadium before the opening ceremony started and athletes from the assorted nations taking part were pleading with me for my drink, as they had not been given any food or water.

Scouts also acted as markers for the marathon and for the 50-km walk. But it was the Sea Scouts who made the greatest contribution. The sailing events took place in Torbay, Devon, and fifty lads from the local area and 150 from further afield ferried competitors with their gear and bags of sails, along with their immediate supporters, to and fro between the boats and jetties. They provided crews for rescue launches, supervised moorings and much more besides. Their eagerness and efficiency did not go unnoticed, and was remarked upon by Crown Prince Olaf of Norway at the closing ceremony.

Boy Scouts were no strangers to fundraising, for as early as May 1914, the Association had organised their first ever nationwide 'good turn' event to raise

Opposite:
Front cover of the
Jubilee issue of *The
Scouter*, July 195

The opening ceremony of the 1948 Olympics, with Senior Scouts carrying the designation boards in front of the flag carrier.

On the opening afternoon of the 1948 Olympics at 4 p.m., hundreds of Scouts sitting around the edge of the crowd released a flock of 7,000 pigeons from 350 large wicker baskets.

funds for the National Institute for the Blind. The scene was set for a much bigger affair, devised by Haydn Dimmock, with the launch of the first official Scout Bob-a-Job week in April 1949, partly to assist 'starving Europe'. Many of the jobs the boys undertook were conventional, like gardening and car washing, but some enterprising Scouts looked for more unusual ways of

earning their money. Not satisfied with shoe-shining on dry land, the boys of 11th St Marylebone troop plied their trade on the cross-channel ferry, *Londoner*, during Bob-a-Job week in 1966. As Hamish Strachan, a ten-year-old member of the 22nd Flintry, remembered: 'We had a card and people wrote their name on it and what job you did and what they paid you and at the end of the week the Scout leader totalled up how much you had made.'

The 1950s were busy years for the Movement. The first post-war Soap Box Derby finals took to the tracks in September 1950, and the event proved so popular that, with one or two exceptions, it became a fixture in the annual Scouting calendar, and in July 1961 was renamed National Scoutcar Races. The Crownhill troop's car failed to make the finals, but demonstrated the ingenuity required in making a vehicle with a limit of fifty shillings for construction materials. Named 'BRJ', which stood for 'bits of rubbish and junk', at the end of the day they took the essential bits of the car back home in a cardboard box, leaving the caretaker to dispose of the rest of the rubbish and junk. Another regular feature returned to the London stage when the lights went up on the Gang Show at the King's Theatre, Hammersmith, in December 1950, with a cast of 150, made up of 'old boys' and new recruits. Reader's concerns that the show would be a financial flop were unfounded, for the audience was more than happy and the show made 'a champion amount of profit'.

The Scouting Movement used the Festival of Britain, officially opened on 3 May 1951, as an ideal opportunity to show the public something of their work. Events included an Antarctic exhibition on RRS *Discovery* on the river Thames, participation in the Pavilion of Youth on London's South Bank, and the provision of an information service for visitors.

Cubs and Scouts from Matlock Green Scout Group polishing shoes in Matlock during Bob-a-Job week, 1950.

One of the Scouts' Antarctic Expedition tableaux, created for the Festival of Britain, 1951.

Two Scouts are sitting in a Slingsby T21 while another connects it to a cable prior to launch at the first Scout Association gliding course at Lasham in 1958. The plane in the background is an AVRO York G-ANTK.

Always prepared, Scouts were on duty at the Coronation of Queen Elizabeth II in June 1952. Having camped out overnight, they assisted with the crowds and sold programmes, whilst their counterparts around the country took part in local processions and fêtes, as well as lighting about 1,400 beacons on Coronation night, stretching from Gallow Hill in the Shetland Islands to St Aubin Fort on Jersey, including twenty-three across Hertfordshire. The new sovereign also gave approval for the most coveted award, the King's Scout Badge, to become the Queen's Scout Badge.

Meanwhile, in October 1950, Air Scout troops were granted permission to apply for Air Ministry recognition and within five years nearly forty troops had achieved the required standard of training and were permitted to wear a special badge and gain experience in service aircraft. The first gliding course for Scouts was made available at Lasham, near Alton in Hampshire, in July 1955. Far less familiar than the land, sea and air Scouts were the Mounted Scouts, with the 1st Hadstock, Essex, having the accolade of being the only mounted troop in Great Britain. Revived as a mounted troop in 1951, they were in demand to give displays at fêtes and carnivals, raising money for good causes with their demonstrations of mounted drill and first aid, jumping and trick-riding. Whilst the mounted Scouts still wore the traditional hat, by 1954 Senior, Rover and Boy Scouts could opt to wear the uniform beret.

The crowning achievement for Reader was the 1954 Gang Show, held at the Golders Green Hippodrome on 9 December, when Her Majesty Queen Elizabeth II came especially to see the entire performance. Some 3,000 people attended, and the young Neville Hurran, who had been chosen to present a bouquet, got so nervous beforehand that he went quite white and had to be revived with a drink of water. The royal backstage tour and compliments on the professionalism of the cast were only surpassed by the Queen's parting words: 'Mr Reader, it has been *wonderful*', making the evening unforgettable in the history of Gang Shows. With Scouting such an international movement, the formation of an International Scout Club, in February 1956, was no great surprise. The Scouts' Golden Jubilee Year, 1957, was also the centenary of B-P's birth, and the year was filled with celebrations. The largest national event was the World Jubilee Jamboree-Indaba-Moot at Sutton Park, Sutton Coldfield, attended by over 30,000 Scouts and Leaders, including one of the Scouts from Pakistan who hiked all the way. The commemorative stamps that were issued created so much interest that the Scout and Guide Stamps Club was set up in July. Local Scout Weeks were held up and down the country, with torchlight processions, long distance walks, pageants and plays. The 145th Glasgow troop marked the events with a service at Glasgow Cathedral and a week-long Scout Show at the Kelvin Hall. And for Scouts who were amateur radio hams – and had passed the Morse Code test which required a speed of twelve words per minute – the first annual Jamboree-on-the-Air was held in October 1958, connecting troops world-wide by radio.

Jock Dawson, Group Scoutmaster of 1st Hadstock troop, Essex, gave tips on how to set about Scouting on horseback in *The Scout's Pathfinder Annual*, 1966.

Nine Scouts of the 1st Coulsdon Group sit around a table learning Morse Code, under the watchful eye of their Scout Leader, c. 1950.

FROM 1960

THE 1960s proved to be an eventful decade for the Scouts, not least of all because of the great changes that were to take place. In June 1963 the Boy Scouts Association took a lease on Lasham airfield, enabling them to provide their own gliding, parascending and ballooning courses. The new Air Activities centre boasted a most unusual 'hut', as John Howard, Scout Leader of the 3rd East Kilbride, who took a party of boys there in the 1970s, recalled. Their dormitory was an old decommissioned de Havilland Comet G-APDK, one of two planes donated by Dan Air; along with an air experience flight in a Cessna, this was part of a big adventure for young teenagers. May 1965 is remembered as the time when the first National Scout Band championships took place, and the 13th Coventry became the Supreme Champions, an achievement that they repeated in the following four years.

As camps and meetings, conferences, activities and outings continued, the Chief Scout's Advance Party Report was published in June 1966. A new Promise and Law were introduced in October 1966 and in May 1967 the Movement changed its name to The Scout Association. Rover and Senior Scouts were replaced by Venture Scouts and Service Teams; Scoutmasters became Scout Leaders; and Wolf Cubs were renamed Cub Scouts. There were new training schemes for Cub Scouts, Scouts and Venture Scouts, and a re-styled Queen's Scout Award became the goal of the new Venture Scout in 1967. Scouting's Diamond Jubilee in 1967 was a great celebration, especially as the membership in the UK had reached an all-time high of 557,918. 1,300 Scouts attended the 12th World Jamboree in Idaho, USA, while at home local districts such as St Albans, put on their own festivities, which included a fireworks display attended by about 6,000 people. As the final issue of *The Scout* went to press in September 1967, Senior and Rover Scouts finally saw the last of short trousers along with the traditional hat. Royalty were still maintaining their links with the Movement, and the young Prince Andrew joined the 1st St Marylebone Cub Scout Pack in January 1968. There were more exciting 'firsts' that year, including the National Scout and Venture Scout Kart Championships

Opposite:
Advertisements
from *The Scouter*,
July 1957.

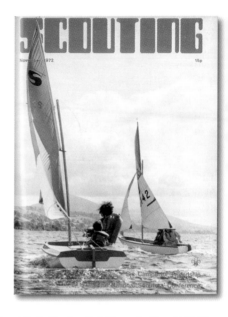

Above and bottom: Advertisements from *The Scouter*, July 1957.

Above right: *Scouting* front cover, November 1972.

and the Scout and Guide National 'Folk Fest' at B-P House in May 1968. The inaugural National Scout CycloCross meeting took place at Gilwell Park, with an obstacle course laid around the perimeter of the grounds. Queen's Guides, celebrating the Girl Guide Movement's Diamond Jubilee Year, joined the annual Queen's Scout Parade at Windsor Castle for the first time.

As the Scouting Movement continued to evolve, and another decade dawned, a new World Membership Badge was introduced in January 1971 for

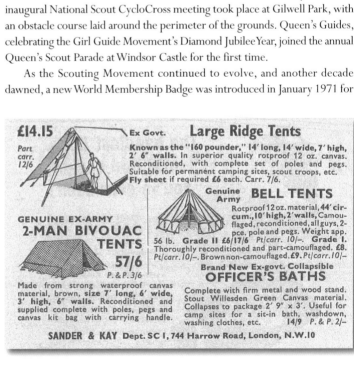

UK Scouts. *The Scouter* acquired a new name, *Scouting*, and notice was given by Lord Maclean, the Chief Scout, of his intended retirement. Folk Fest was so successful that the venue changed twice, moving first to the 1,900-seater Fairfield Concert Hall in Croydon, in February 1970, and then to the Royal Albert Hall. The event in December 1973 was compèred by Terry Wogan, and attended by nearly 6,000 people, who were entertained by top Scout and Guide folk music artists and groups from all over the UK, as well as three from the continent. The final curtain came down on the London Gang Show in 1974, when Reader, aged 71, decided to retire, but the tradition he had established endured. Scouts in towns and cities up and down the UK, and as far afield as New Zealand and Australia, continued to put on innovative shows, displaying creativity and talent. All around the world Scouts have benefited from Reader's generosity in allowing them free use of his songs and sketches, with between £2 million and £3 million raised for local funds. The success of the Scoutreach Campaign, launched in 1975, proved that it was possible to reach out to boys in deprived areas (like the project run in St Mark's, near Leicester, for example), and enable them to gain self-respect and a sense of purpose.

By the summer of 1980, UK Scout membership had reached 641,281. The National Air Activities Centre at Lasham closed in March 1980, but Air Scouting carried on, giving Scouts the opportunity of learning aeronautical

The finale of the last London Gang Show, 1974.

Help The Scouts

And Help Stop The Rot

Scouts

skills and undertaking flight training. The 4th Tolworth Air Scouts, formed in 1941, was re-awarded prestigious RAF recognition in 2007, allowing its Scouts to participate in week-long camps in Gloucestershire with RAF pilots. 1982 was another important milestone in Scouting history, for it was the 75th Anniversary of Brownsea Island camp. The year was designated 'The Year of the Scout', and was launched at a House of Commons reception by the Speaker, attended by seventy-five famous former Scouts and other Scout representatives. More than eighty countries issued special postage stamps, and the celebration challenge was to include

Driven by social need, the Scoutreach campaign, initiated and led by the Chief Scout, Sir William Gladstone, set out to bring Scouting to areas of deprivation where it was either non-existent, or struggling to survive.

A group of Scouts preparing to fly their hot air balloon displaying The Scout Association emblem. Gilwell Park, 1976.

'seventy-five' in every activity. Events included parties organised for seventy-five elderly people, there were Scouts tidying up seventy-five square yards of land while the 6th Boston fed seventy-five pigs. Now on the scene was another section of Scouting, this time for younger boys between six and eight years old, with a programme of fun and learning suited to their age. Beavers, as they were called, had to wait until 1986 to become an official part of the Scouting family, as Beaver Scouts.

Badge celebrating the Year of the Scout, 1982.

There were casualties in the 1980s as interest in some activities declined, and both Folk Fest and national CycloCross disappeared from the Scouting calendar. But county CycloCross events and National Trek Cart races continued to flourish, with participation in the latter requiring ingenuity and perseverance. The eighteen Scout teams who entered the races in the New Forest in summer 1989 had to run with their carriage, dismantle it, and cross an obstacle course before rebuilding it and running to the finish. The winners, the 2nd Aldershot Venture Scout Unit, completed the gun carriage race in 1 minute, 42 seconds, 21 seconds faster than any other team.

Another decade brought further change and innovation, especially when, in 1991, the decision was made to allow girls to be members of all sections of the Scouts. The following year, the 'Monopoly Run' was introduced for Venture Scouts and proved to be a great adventure, with groups racing around the capital, solving clues and getting proof of their visit to all the London Monopoly sites. In a break with tradition, George Purdy, who was appointed the eighth Chief Scout in March 1996, was a civil servant with no military background, but a wealth of Scouting experience. To commemorate eighty years of Cub Scouting, the Cubs took their lead from Jules Verne, and in August 1996 started eighty days of special events, including a nationwide challenge to 'travel round the world' in eighty days. Embracing the latest technology, the *Jamboree-on-the-Internet* joined *JOTA* as an official event of the World Organization of the Scout Movement in November 1996.

Scouts of all sections in their new uniform, designed by Meg Andrews, in front of the Gidney Cabin at Gilwell Park, 2001.

THE TWENTY-FIRST CENTURY

THE NEW CENTURY got off to a flying start for UK Scouts as they took part in the Millennium Chase. Besides the introduction of a millennium badge and song, a series of events held during 2000 included weekend camps, many of which were remembered for the mud and rain. In 2001, HQ operations, previously split between Gilwell Park and Baden-Powell House (South Kensington) were combined at Gilwell, and a new logo and uniform was introduced for the UK's 500,000 Scouts. But what remained unchanged were the scarf and World Badge, which continue to unite Scouts across the world. Even though the last National Scout Band Festival was held in 2001, Scout bands, like the 1st Hook Scout and Guide Band, founded in 1938, continue to flourish, playing at local, national and international events throughout the year, and raising money for group funds.

New Scout logo, 2001.

A Scout Band member at Windsor Castle, 2006.

Even greater changes came in 2002. A new youth programme was introduced along with a change in age ranges. Venture Scouts were replaced with Explorer Scouts for those aged fourteen to eighteen, and a new dynamic Scout Network, for eighteen- to twenty-five-year-olds, gave the older group far more autonomy and responsibility. Exciting activities such as kayaking, orienteering and climbing are the norm, as well as the opportunity of working on local community projects and with younger Scouting groups. The appointment of TV presenter, Peter Duncan, as the ninth Chief Scout in 2004, was inspirational, for although he had no significant Scouting background, many more young people were attracted to the Movement under his leadership. A nationwide campaign, 'Gimmie 5', was launched in 2005 to raise funds and awareness of the work of The Scout Association and the World Wildlife Fund, with much of the money raised by groups diverted to help victims of the tsunami in Southern Asia.

These Scouts were attending a mass lobby at the House of Commons on 15 July 2009, as part of the Scout Association 'Stop the Rain Tax' campaign. The former Rugby international, Brian Moore, is pictured on the far right.

Explorer Scouts trying out some off-road skateboarding at Gilwell 24 in July 2008. This annual twenty-four hour activity event at Gilwell Park was introduced in 2005.

In July 2007, a century after B-P held the first experimental camp on Brownsea Island, some 40,000 young people from 158 countries attended the twenty-first World Scout Jamboree at Hylands Park near Chelmsford, Essex, a testament to his vision that Scouting could transcend race, religion and country. Many of those were able to attend because of more than £10,000 raised by UK Scouts for the World Friendship Appeal, as part of the

UK Chief Scout,
Bear Grylls, 2010.

Prince William
visiting the 21st
World Scout
Jamboree at
Hylands Park,
Essex in summer
2007.

2006 Gimmie 5 campaign. There are now more than 100,000 Wood Badge recipients worldwide, and since 1952 well over 45,000 Queen's Scout Awards have been presented to young men and women.

As an addition to the formal Scout uniform, a casual range of i.Scout clothing was designed in 2008, widening the appeal of Scouting and its opportunities. Yet another move away from tradition was made in July 2009, when the adventurer, Bear Grylls, began his five-year tenure as UK Chief Scout, for he was the youngest person ever to hold the post.

Being involved as one of 250 official Scout programme sellers at the wedding of Prince William in April 2011 was especially thrilling for Robert, a sixteen-year-old Explorer Scout from Woolwich, London. His grandfather, Robert Gammon, had done the same as a Scout at the wedding of the Queen,

then Princess Elizabeth. He said, 'I'm proud to be doing the same thing my granddad did, sixty-four years later. He had a collection box, and I've got an apron, but it's great to see all these people and feel like you're part of it.' Beaver Scouts across the country celebrated their twenty-fifth anniversary in 2011, and East Grinstead District marked the occasion by planting a small wood of twenty-five trees, and enjoyed tea and a cake decorated with the commemorative badge.

In late 2011 there were 400,000 Scouts in the UK, aged from six to twenty-five, with another 30,000 on waiting lists. While there are over 100,000 volunteers who make Scouting possible, there is still an urgent need for more young people to help out. By giving some of her time to help local Scouts, the Duchess of Cambridge, the newest royal to support The Scout Association, hopes to serve as a role model for others. Bob-a-Job week ended in the 1990s, but in 2012 UK Scouts will be encouraged by The Scout Association to volunteer to do work to help their local community during Scout Community Week.

Sporting the new i.Scout tops, 2009.

Members can now download an app on to their mobile phone, which provides them with all the badge requirements.

Scouts across the world take part in educational, environmental and health projects and often play a vital role in disaster relief, including recovery and rebuilding work following the Asian tsunami in 2005, and providing support for the charity, Shelterbox, who supplied important aid following the Haiti earthquake.

One hundred years after the Scouting Movement was given its Royal Charter, it continues to be a unique organisation, and is remarkable in the way it has grown from B-P's experimental camp in 1907 to achieve global popularity. It has constantly moved with the times, embraced technology and ensured that it remains relevant to the youth of today and modern society. Importantly, this has been achieved without compromising the fundamental principles of fun, friendship, adventure and good deeds laid down by its visionary founder all those years ago.

FURTHER READING

Baden-Powell, Robert (author) and Boehmer, Elleke (ed.). *Scouting for Boys: A Handbook for Instruction in Good Citizenship.* Oxford University Press, 2004. A reproduction of the original 1908 edition, with a new introduction.

Harris, Steven. *Baden-Powell's Footprint across Britain.* Lewarne, 2010.

Harris, Steven. *Baden-Powell Country: Scouting Footprints, Places and Plaques.* Lewarne, 2011.

Masini, Roy. *Sea Scouting: A History, 1909–2009.* Phillimore, 2011. The most comprehensive study of the history of sea scouting.

The Scout Association with a foreword by Lord Robert Baden-Powell. *An Official History of Scouting.* Hamlyn, 2006.

Walker, Colin. *The Dawn of the World Scout Movement.* Scouting Milestones, 2008. About the first troops and Humshaugh camp.

Walker, Colin. *Brownsea: B-P's Acorn.* Scouting Milestones, 2008. The story of the Experimental Camp in 1907.

Walker, Colin. *Scouting Collectables,* Vols I and II. Scouting Milestones, 2010 and 2011. Highly illustrated books dealing with scouting ephemera and memorabilia.

(Colin Walker's books are available from www.scouting.milestones.btinternet.co.uk)

WEBSITES

The official Scout Association website has a wealth of information about all aspects of the organisation (www.scouts.org.uk).

The Scout Association Archive acts as the custodian of the Scout Association's and Baden-Powell's family historical memories, and includes archive material, library, audio-visual items, fine art, museum objects and structures. (By prior arrangement only.) Archive & Heritage Department, The Scout Association, Gilwell Park, London E4 7QW. Telephone: 020 8433 7195. Fax: 020 8433 7103. Website: www.scoutsrecords.org.

The Scout Association Scotland has its own website, www.scouts-scotland.org.uk, as does Scouting Ireland, www.scouts.ie/ and Scouts Wales, www.scoutswales.org.uk.

Colin Walker's website (www.scouting.milestones.btinternet.co.uk) has a wealth of information on worldwide Scout history.

The National Register of Archives (www.nationalarchives.gov.uk): documents in record offices and elsewhere relating to numerous local Scout Associations.

Archives Wales, 'Scouts and scouting' (www.archiveswales.org.uk): papers
relating to various Welsh Scouting Associations.
The National Archives of Scotland (www.nas.gov.uk): documents in record
offices and elsewhere relating to the BSA and numerous Scout
Associations.

PLACES TO VISIT

Gilwell Park Estate. Guided heritage tours of the Gilwell Park estate, as
well as exclusive tours of the archive stores, can be organised. (By prior
arrangement only.) Archive & Heritage Department, The Scout
Association, Gilwell Park, London, E4 7QW.
Telephone: 020 8433 7195. Fax: 020 8433 7103.
Hertfordshire County Scout Museum and Archive Cabin, County HQ,
Well End Activity Centre, Well End, Borehamwood, Hertfordshire
WD6 5PR. County Archivist: Frank Brittain. (Visits by appointment
only.) Telephone: 0845 643 6973.
Email: archivist@hertfordshirescouts.org.uk.
Story of Scouting Museum, Waddecar Scout Activity Centre, Snape Rake
Lane, Goosnargh, Preston, Lancashire PR3 2EU. Curator: Michael
Loomes. Telephone: 01995 61336.
Website: www.storyofscouting.org.uk.

INDEX

Page numbers in italics refer to illustrations